DISCARDED

## DATE DUE

| | | | |
|---|---|---|---|
| | | | |
| | | | |
| | | | |
| | | | |
| | | | |
| | | | |
| | | | |
| | | | |
| | | | |
| | | | |
| | | | |
| | | | |
| | | | |

# DAIRY
# COUNTRY

# BY LYNN M. STONE

THE ROURKE CORPORATION, INC.
Vero Beach, FL 32964

Edited by Sandra A. Robinson

## PHOTO CREDITS

All photos © Lynn M. Stone except photo on page 10 courtesy of W.D. Hoard and Sons Company

## ACKNOWLEDGEMENTS

Pat and Phyllis Agnew, Jim and Carole Boesche, Sid Cook, John Dalton, Tim Duren, Tom Holak, Nelson Lee, Mary Luckhardt, Kathy Luttropp, Steve Schulenburg, Gaylord Schroeder, Wes Seffrood, Dan and Diane Serge, Devon Slaybaw and Brian Voegeli

## DEDICATION

For the Dairy Farmers of Wisconsin and Their "Girls"

**Library of Congress Cataloging-in-Publication Data**
Stone, Lynn M.
    Dairy country / by Lynn M. Stone.
      p. cm. – (Back roads)
    Includes index.
    Summary: An introduction to the dairy farming industry of Wisconsin.
    ISBN 0-86593-302-2
    1. Dairy farming—Wisconsin—Juvenile literature. 2. Dairy farms—Wisconsin—Juvenile literature. 3. Farm life—Wisconsin—Juvenile literature. [1. Dairying—Wisconsin.] I. Title II. Series: Stone, Lynn M. Back roads.
SF239.5.S85  1993
636.2'142'09775—dc20                      93-13503
                                          CIP
                                          AC

Printed in the USA

# TABLE OF CONTENTS

**BACK ROADS**

## CHAPTER 1

# DAIRY COUNTRY

Wisconsin is dairy country. Wisconsin's auto license plates proclaim – "America's Dairyland." Believe them. A person can travel almost anywhere in Wisconsin, outside of downtown Milwaukee, and expect to see at least bits of dairyland, the farm country where milk-producing cattle – "milking cows" – are raised. In many parts of Wisconsin, however, all the land seems to be dairyland.

*Wisconsin dairy country from "upstairs" in Sauk County*

*Dairy farm in the stillness of Wisconsin winter*

To really "taste" dairy country, climb "upstairs."
Wisconsin didn't grow mountains, but it has plenty of
hills where the ancient glaciers didn't grind and scour the
earth flat. Climb a hill in, say, Sauk County, near
Reedsburg. Then gaze around and sniff the wind.
Dairyland spreads before you in a chessboard of barns,
pastures, contoured fields, brushy fence rows and squares
of forest where sugar maples and birches mingle. It is all
laid out like a colorful painting just the way American
farm country is supposed to look, and the way it must have
looked 50 or 60 or 70 years ago. A painting it just might
be, except the little, distant knots of cattle move. And

*Wisconsin leads the nation in dairy cows, most of them black and white Holsteins*

they gossip and bellow with *moos* that the wind lifts to your ears. The same wind blows the earthy fragrances of dairy country. It may be the scent of cut alfalfa one day or the pungent smell of fertilizer the next. Both are plentiful in dairy country.

Milking cows and the farms that shelter them are familiar sights in some other parts of the United States, too. California, New York, Minnesota and Pennsylvania have strong dairying traditions and large herds of milking cows. But Wisconsin is special. Dairy farming has not been restricted to a small part of Wisconsin. For generations, dairying has been a family tradition and livelihood throughout the state.

As anyone who has visited the state in July knows, more mosquitoes populate Wisconsin than dairy cattle. More people – about 5 million – reside in Wisconsin than dairy cattle. But, Wisconsin has 1,750,000 dairy cattle – far more than any other state and more than 17 percent of the nation's total. One of every six dairy cows in America has a Wisconsin address. With so many dairy cattle, no wonder that Wisconsin leads the nation in milk production. The state's milking cows produce about 148 billion pounds of milk annually, or some 16.5 percent of the nation's entire milk production. Wisconsin also produces more cheese than any other state, nearly one-third of all cheese made in America.

Wisconsin has more pounds of dairy cattle than pounds of people. Yet, contrary to what some people in neighbor state Illinois believe, not everyone in Wisconsin milks cows, makes cheese or mends fences. Only a small percentage of Wisconsin residents are directly involved with the dairy industry. Nevertheless, dairying has left its imprint on Wisconsin life. A store owner moving to a new Wisconsin location raised this message on a billboard: "Herd about our Moo look?" A Wisconsin lottery suggested that buying a ticket might make the buyer "More Moolah." In Wisconsin, cows are part of the culture.

## CHAPTER 2
# DAIRY COUNTRY HISTORY

*Wisconsin's family dairy tradition began in the 19th century*

Dairy cattle didn't just horn their way into Wisconsin life and lotteries overnight. The process began – quite slowly – when milking cows were brought to the state by the first Europeans who settled in Wisconsin. That was more than 150 years ago. Large numbers of the settlers were Czech, German, English, French and Irish. They were neither strangers to farming nor to dairy cattle.

*William Dempster Hoard was a leading Wisconsin dairyman in the late 19th century and founder of* Hoard's Dairyman

While they didn't rush into dairy farming, they did find Wisconsin a likely place to re-establish other **agricultural, or farming,** traditions. The settlers found abundant land with gentle terrain, and they pitched into the work of making it farm-ready. They plowed up the prairies where wild grasses grew tall and deep. They hacked away forest. The soil under their feet was not as rich as the incredibly black earth of Iowa and Illinois, but it was fertile. The settlers scattered seeds and their fields sprang to life with wheat, clover, alfalfa and straw.

By 1870, Wisconsin was an established "farm state," but industry was becoming increasingly important. Along the big lakes several industrial communities had rooted – Manitowoc, Fond du Lac, Milwaukee, Green Bay and others. At the same time, some of the wheat-producing farms faltered. Nonstop wheat production was sapping the relatively thin topsoil's **nutrients,** or nourishing ingredients. The wheat harvests had grown progressively lighter. Farmers were beginning to abandon fields and homes.

William Dempster Hoard was a keen observer of the Wisconsin farm scene in the 1870s. He was a man of considerable vision, intellect, compassion and initiative. These were all qualities that Mr. Hoard would need when he began a one-man crusade to change and improve farming practices in Wisconsin. Mr. Hoard recalled that farming had once been on the decline in New York state. It had been rescued when farmers switched from large-scale production of crops to dairy farming. Mr. Hoard encouraged Wisconsin farmers not to desert agriculture altogether, but to eliminate unprofitable crops and poor farming practices. Their best alternative, he suggested, was to raise dairy cattle.

*This Ayrshire and her herd may mow grass to the ground, but the grass will recover*

Mr. Hoard explained that cattle would offer a profitable and soil-conserving approach to agriculture. Cattle would mow the grass to the ground, but the grass would grow back, fertilized by the cows' droppings. Lost nutrients would be promptly returned to the soil.

Some farmers, of course, were already raising dairy cattle. They were soon joined by others. The growth of industrial cities created a market for dairy products, and the use of ice-cooled freight cars made transportation of fresh milk possible over fairly long distances.

Mr. Hoard himself, always enthusiastic, established a herd of Guernsey cattle in Fort Atkinson, Wisconsin. He formed the Wisconsin Dairymen's Association and founded an important magazine, *Hoard's Dairyman.* Mr. Hoard used his own herd to demonstrate improved farming techniques and convince doubters that dairying could be permanent and profitable. Meanwhile, *Hoard's Dairyman,* first published in 1885, grew to be one of the most progressive and respected dairy publications in the world.

By 1890, much of the Wisconsin countryside had been converted to dairy farming. William D. Hoard was the governor of Wisconsin, and the University of Wisconsin at Madison established the nation's first dairy school. The

*The growth of industrial cities helped create a growing market for Wisconsin's dairy farms*

herds of dairy cattle – Jerseys, brown Swiss, Guernseys, Holsteins and Ayrshires – continued to grow. By 1925, Wisconsin had nearly 2 million dairy cattle. The number of Wisconsin dairy cows climbed to more than 2,300,000 during World War II (1939-1945). By then, there were two milking cows for every three people.

In the decades after World War II, milk prices did not keep pace with the farmers' costs. The nation's population grew, but its taste for dairy products didn't. Dairy farmers found that they needed larger herds to make a profit. The size of the average dairy herd in Wisconsin jumped from about 37 in 1977 to 53 in 1990. An expanding line of farm machinery helped reduce the farmers' work load and allow them to raise more cattle. Although more efficient, the new machinery was also expensive and created some massive debts for farmers.

Between 1951 and 1990, the number of Wisconsin dairy farms fell from 132,000 to 33,000. Debt, low-profit and no-profit operations forced some farmers to quit. Changing lifestyles played a role, too. Modern farm machinery is powerful and efficient, but someone still has to rise with the rooster and milk the cows. Many young people in dairyland, after thinking about the long hours and hard labor of dairying, began to look for their futures elsewhere.

"Mom and Pop" dairy farms haven't vanished from Wisconsin. Dairy farming is still done largely by individual, independent families whose Wisconsin roots are as deep as the oak's in the front yard. In fact, signboards at many farm homes tell a traveler exactly who Mom and Pop are. But fewer Mom and Pop dairy farms

*The sun begins to rise, along with the rooster and dairy farmer, on a September morning*

will weather the future. Mom and Pop already raise larger herds and farm more acres than their ancestors did. Eventually, it may take more than a family farm to turn milk into gold as well as butter.

## Chapter 3

# PASTURES AND PRAIRIES, WOODLANDS AND WETLANDS

*Many of dairyland's old, wooden barns are traditional red*

*Early autumn mist cloaks a wetland and dairy pasture*

Dairy farms are scattered from one end of Wisconsin to the other. The great majority are in the lower three-quarters of the state. Some dairy barns stand on hilltops and in valleys, while others rise from table-flat plains. The only hills their cows ever climb are the ramps leading to the stalls. A few dairy farms have been carved out of the spruce and pine forests of northern Wisconsin.

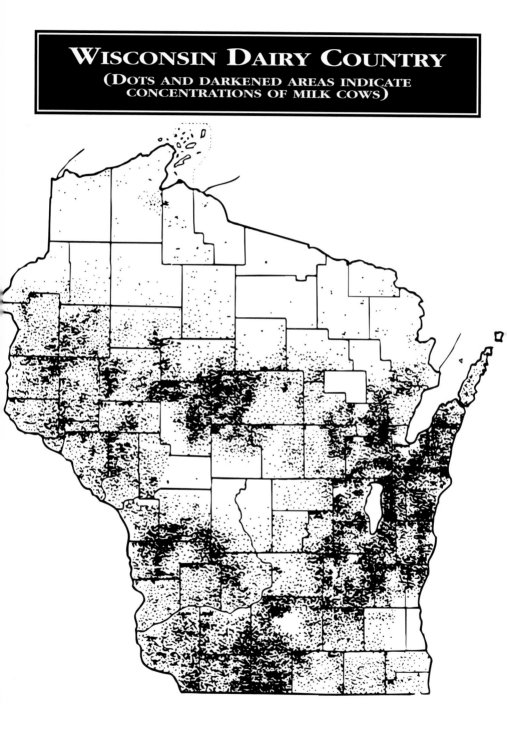

# WISCONSIN DAIRY COUNTRY
### (DOTS AND DARKENED AREAS INDICATE
### CONCENTRATIONS OF MILK COWS)

Old, wooden cattle barns are still familiar sights in Wisconsin dairy country. Most of them are red or white; fewer are cream-colored, gray or green. Some are freshly-painted, still strong. They have weathered 60 or even 80 years of use. Other barns, now abandoned, have collapsed into jumbles of timbers.

Dairy farms share the Wisconsin countryside with about 15,000 lakes, and great tracts of woodlands and wetlands. Whitetailed-deer, red foxes and squirrels are common there, and wolves have returned to the northern woods. The lakes and marshes attract thousands of ducks, geese and tundra swans each spring and fall.

The Wisconsin outdoors attracts hundreds of thousands of tourists each year, too. They come mostly to ski, swim, raft the rivers, hunt and fish. They don't visit Wisconsin purposely to gaze at pretty-as-a-picture dairy pastures and grazing dairy cattle. But dairy country keeps winning new admirers. With remarkably good humor, dairy farmers tolerate tourists who trespass a step or two and point cameras at cattle and barns. Perhaps the tourists sense they are photographing an American scene that may disappear long before their pictures fade.

CHAPTER 4

# LIFE ON THE DAIRY FARM

A dairy farmer may be short of cash or cattle, straw or corn – but the farmer is never short of work. If you raise dairy cows, you milk them twice a day – around dawn and again 12 hours later. The barn may be groaning in a blizzard and a farmer's teeth may be chattering. Or a farmer may be sweat-wet through overalls in a barn where the humidity is high enough to nurture a rain forest. No matter what, the farmer must milk the cows.

During milking, dairy farmers keep their cattle in **stanchions** – steel braces that fit loosely around a cow's neck. Other farmers keep cows on rope leads in tie stalls. In milking parlors, cattle are milked on elevated platforms so that the farmer can stand rather than kneel.

Some of Wisconsin's Amish people farm traditionally and milk their cows by hand. The vast majority of dairy cattle are milked by electric milking machines. The machine draws milk from the cow's **udder,** or milk bag, and pumps it through a pipeline into a container. The milk is stored and cooled in a tank until it is collected by truck and shipped to a processing plant. While one cow is

*Dairy farmer attaches milking machine to the udder of a purebred Guernsey*

being milked, the farmer moves quickly to another and prepares her for milking by washing her udder with a **disinfectant,** or germ-killer. The milking machine takes about five minutes to empty an udder. The cow gives anywhere from 20 to 40 pounds of milk at each milking. The breed, time of year and individual cow are all factors that affect the quantity of milk.

*A cow such as this Holstein can drink 35 gallons of water and eat 100 pounds of food in a day*

The farmer who milks an average herd spends about two hours at each milking session. Milking, however, is just one of the farmer's barn chores. The farmer distributes cattle feed and straw bedding, rinses and cleans milking utensils, and keeps feed and milk records. The farmer also has to remove cow **manure,** or waste, from the barn. A cow can consume up to 100 pounds of food and drink 35 gallons of water per day. She produces a large quantity of manure.

A dairy farmer's work only begins in the barn. Beyond the barns lie the fields that produce grass and cattle food crops. Always with an eye on the weather, the dairy farmer has to fertilize, plow, disc, seed, cultivate and harvest the crops. Harvests are particularly critical times. Heavy rains and droughts can ruin crops. Once a crop has been gathered, it has to be properly stored, usually in silos.

The machines farmers use to work the fields – tractors, **combines** and other implements – have to be kept in running condition. That often means adding another title – "mechanic" – to the dairy farmer's job description. It's a list that already includes animal doctor, soil doctor, nutritionist, accountant, electrician, weather forecaster, barn painter and agriculture student.

The hard work of dairy farming has its dividends, although they are not always bankable. The only wealthy farmers, says one, are in the cemetery. Valuable farmland is converted into cash only after the farmer's death, in many cases. The greatest dividend may be that dairy farmers generally enjoy their work. Working with animals and earth gives dairy farmers a satisfaction with their labors that most people never know. That may help explain why dairylanders are such an unassuming, friendly and industrious group.

*Field crops surround a Holstein farm near Reedsburg, Wisconsin*

CHAPTER 5

# COWS ARE COOL

*"The rule to be observed in this stable at all times, toward the cattle, young and old, is that of patience and kindness. A man's usefulness in a herd ceases at once when he loses his temper and bestows rough usage. Men must be patient. Cattle are not reasoning beings. Remember that this is the Home of Mothers. Treat each cow as a Mother should be treated. The giving of milk is a function of Motherhood; rough treatment lessens the flow. That injures me as well as the cow. Always keep these things in mind in dealing with my cattle."*

—**William D. Hoard**

*This Jersey with her wet muzzle and curious nature is about to introduce herself to the photographer*

24

*Even children sense the gentleness of cows, like this 1,100-pound Guernsey*

Dairy country would not exist without the big, hoofed creatures we call cattle. Spanish explorers brought the first cattle to North America in the 1500s. Wisconsin probably had no resident cattle until the first European settlers trickled to the area in the 1700s.

Female cattle – cows – are generally curious, good-natured and easy-going. They spend most of their time eating, resting and chewing. Like slobbery dogs, they have long, raspy tongues and wet muzzles. Once a cow makes your acquaintance, she'll use both tongue and muzzle to "say hello."

A Holstein cow can weigh 1,500 pounds, and even a "little" Jersey can weigh 1,000 pounds. That kind of bulk should be intimidating to small, smarter creatures, but even little kids seem to know that cows are gentle. Cows don't terrorize anyone – and everyone likes a gentle giant. Cows are the subjects of crafts, calendars, puzzles, curtains and wallpaper. Cows are cool.

Our modern-day cool cows are the descendants of the aurochs, a **species,** or kind, of wild cattle once found in Europe and Asia. The aurochs became extinct in 1627, leaving four species of wild cattle – the banteng, guar, kouprey and yak – all of them in Asia.

The aurochs was a long-haired, long-horned animal that didn't look like most of its descendants – with good reason. For about 8,000 years, farmers have been raising cattle selectively. Once people decided to keep herds of wild cattle and **domesticate,** or tame them, they selected certain characteristics of the animals to keep or improve. A cow with a particularly large udder, for example, provided more milk than other cows. The farmer would select her for **breeding,** or reproducing, in hopes that her calves would be more outstanding milk producers than calves from cows with smaller udders. Eventually several pure **breeds,** or types, of domestic cattle were established. Some of them did have a tremendous capacity for milk. Yet without the involvement of people, that would not have happened. Nature alone would never have lent her hand to developing udders that, when full, nearly drag the ground.

*Long-haired, long-horned Scotch highland cattle are smaller, but similar to the aurochs, the wild ancestor of modern dairy breeds*

*All dairy cattle are basically the same kind of animal, whether they are milking shorthorns (left), Holsteins (right) or some other breed*

Selective breeding is an ongoing process. Agricultural scientists are continually working to improve breeds. Today's cow is healthier and can have a calf (baby cow) sooner because she grows up faster on improved foods. For the same reasons, a **heifer,** or young cow, is more likely than ever to be a good milk producer. Her food is better, and a farmer has chosen her ancestors carefully. The

average cow today gives three times more milk than the average cow of 1940.

All domestic cattle are basically the same animal, *Bos taurus.* They all grow hollow horns, have the same kind of hoofs, and share the same layout of teeth and body organs. They simply vary in overall size, color and body shape. Some are hardier than others, too.

*This Ayrshire lass is polled for the safety of the farmer and the other cows in her herd*

Nearly every breed has a distinct color or pattern of colors, and each milking breed produces milk that varies in its quantity and butterfat (cream) content. Today most cattle are **polled,** or dehorned, to prevent injuries to both farmers and other cattle. However, cattle breeds show distinct differences in horns when they are allowed to grow.

Most of Wisconsin's dairy herds are **purebred.** All the cattle in a herd belong to the same breed. More than nine of every 10 Wisconsin dairy cattle are black and white Holsteins. Holsteins are the biggest dairy cattle and produce the most milk. The average Holstein cow gives nearly 15,000 pounds of milk each year. Nearly all of the other purebred Wisconsin herds are Guernseys, Jerseys, brown Swiss and Ayrshires.

*"Golden" Guernseys were nicknamed for their creamy, golden milk and their golden-brown color*

Jerseys are small, brownish cattle with short, broad faces. They give the richest milk. Brown Swiss are large cattle that originated in Switzerland. Their milk is particularly desirable to cheese manufacturers. Guernseys are golden brown and white. Next to Jerseys, they give the creamiest milk. Ayrshire cattle, an English breed, are reddish-brown and white. The average Ayrshire cow will produce more milk than Guernseys or Jerseys, but less than Holsteins and brown Swiss.

*Fresh snow brings out the kid in these Ayrshire cows*

Like their human bosses, cattle are hardy. Their hair thickens in winter, and they can withstand Wisconsin winter temperatures of zero degrees Fahrenheit as long as they have straw bedding and no wind. On moderately cold days, dairy cattle are routinely let out of the barn for fresh air and exercise. With the enthusiasm of school children, dairy cows sometimes bound through barnyard snow.

Dairy herds in Wisconsin can graze in pastures from May through October. After munching grass for awhile, cattle lie down and chew their **cuds.** A cow has 170 feet of intestine, four stomach chambers and a complex system of digestion. Part of the process is **regurgitation,** or bringing up partially digested food from the stomach for another chewing. This new version of the old meal is called the cud.

The dairy farmer supplements the grass diet of grazing cattle with prepared foods. On a growing number of Wisconsin dairy farms, cattle live strictly on a diet provided by the farmer. The cattle are confined to the barn and barnyard. Their feed is often a ready-made mix of cornmeal, soybean meal, grains, cotton seed, beet pulp and other nutrients. On the most modern dairy farms, computers calculate the proper mix and amount of food for each cow. Healthy cows can be raised on food from a bag, as well as food directly from a pasture.

*A brown Swiss miss, chewing her cud, passes a cool September morning*

Dairy cattle can live more than 20 years, but their life expectancy is usually decided by the farmer. Farming is a business, and dairy cattle are expensive to raise. Cows earn their room and board by producing milk and calves. When a cow's milk production sags, she is sold for stew meat. She is then replaced by a younger, more productive cow. (Farm pickup trucks meet the same fate.) A cow may produce healthy calves and a steady volume of milk until she is 15 or 16 years old. A majority of cows, however, stop producing efficiently after the age of 10 or 12 years.

*Dairy cows on this modern Wisconsin farm are raised strictly on nutritious, prepared foods rather than on pasture forage*

A cow doesn't give milk until she has her first calf. A heifer usually calves between the ages of 27 and 33 months. The calf is raised independently of its mother after being given some of its mother's milk, which has disease-fighting **antibodies.** Two months after calving, a cow is again made pregnant. She will continue to give milk, except for short intervals when she is "dry," throughout her lifetime.

The life expectancy of a bull calf is usually measured in days. The farmer sells a dairy bull calf almost immediately for **veal,** as young beef is called. Just a few bull calves are raised to adulthood and used to father cattle. A small number of Holstein bull calves are raised as **steers** and sold for beef.

Many dairy farmers do not keep a bull. Dairy bulls tend to be short-tempered and dangerous. Even a "good-natured" bull is potentially dangerous because of its enormous size. Bulls often top 2,000 pounds.

*By tugging the ring in this Guernsey bull's sensitive nose, the farmer can usually direct the bull's movements*

CHAPTER 6

# FROM COW TO CARTON

When you buy milk, it is **pasteurized,** and it may be **homogenized.** But that's not the way the cow brought it back from the pasture. A cow delivers "whole" milk, a mixture of cream (butterfat), milk and small milk solids. Milk processing plants separate whole milk into its various parts. Then an entire range of dairy products can be produced, including butter, cheese, ice cream, ice milk, cream, yogurt, cottage cheese, sour cream, buttermilk and dried milk. One pound of butter, for example, requires 21 pounds of whole milk.

*Milk leaves a Wisconsin dairy farm in a stainless steel truck bound for a processing plant*

*Workmen divide sections of cheese at the Carr Valley Cheese Factory in Lavalle, Wisconsin*

When whole milk is homogenized – blended under great pressure – the cream is evenly distributed throughout. People who want to reduce their intake of fats often buy skim milk, which contains no cream.

Today's milk products are distributed in carefully packaged cartons, bottles, cans and boxes. In the early days of Wisconsin dairying, milk was hauled around in cans. Families filled their pitchers with milk that was sometimes infected by diseases, such as tuberculosis. Butter was even less appetizing. It was sometimes sour from the lack of refrigeration. Occasionally it contained vegetable oils and melted cattle fat, or **tallow.** Now milk is pasteurized – heated at a high temperature – to kill unwanted bacteria.

## CHAPTER 7

# DAIRY COUNTRY IN THE 21ST CENTURY

*Dairying lingers as an enduring and engaging way of life in rural Wisconsin*

Dairy farms in Wisconsin will undoubtedly continue to grow in size but dwindle in number. To be profitable, a farmer will have to raise more cattle. It's also likely that fewer people will want to join the dairy ranks. The dairy farmer's schedule is increasingly unappealing to young people as a lifetime career.

Perhaps the time will come when most Wisconsin dairies will be owned by corporations, and their vast herds will be confined indoors, like chickens. Computers will select and release meal packets, the TV dinners of the cattle set. Maybe robots will nimbly attach milking machines. By then, the sighting of dairy cattle freed in a pasture will create traffic jams, as grizzlies in Yellowstone do.

Meanwhile, Wisconsin dairy country lingers as more than just a place. It remains, for the moment at least, as an enduring, engaging way of life.

# GLOSSARY

**agricultural** – of or related to farming

**antibodies** – natural substances in the body that fight disease

**breed** – a particular type of domestic animal with characteristics that separate it clearly from other animals of the same kind (*Holstein* cattle as distinct from *Guernsey* cattle)

**breeding** – the process of animal reproduction

**combine** – a type of large harvesting machine that gathers various grains

**cud** – the food brought up into the mouth of certain plant-eating animals for re-chewing

**disinfectant** – a germ-killing agent

**domesticate** – the process by which certain wild animals are modified in their behavior and appearance for raising and use by people

**heifer** – among cattle, a young female that has not had a calf

**homogenized** – the process by which the ingredients of whole milk are uniformly blended together under pressure

**manure** – the solid waste products of digestion from domestic animals

**nutrients** – ingredients with great value as nourishment

**pasteurize** – to heat at a high temperature to destroy harmful organisms, especially in milk

**polled** – to have had the horns removed

**purebred** – a domestic animal of a single, pure breed

**regurgitation** – the process of bringing up partially digested food from within the body

**species** – a group of plants or animals whose members reproduce naturally only with other members of the same group; a particular kind of plant or animal, such as *aurochs* cattle being separate from *banteng* cattle

**stanchion** – a metal device that fits loosely around the neck of a cow or bull, and limits forward and backward motion

**steer** – among cattle, a male that has had its reproductive organs removed and is raised for meat

**tallow** – melted animal fat

**udder** – the large, sagging body part that encloses a cow's milk-producing glands; the milk bag

**veal** – the meat of a calf

# INDEX

# INDEX